EVERYDAY ETIQUETTE

EVERYDAY ETIQUETTE

Everyday Etiquette

Polite Behaviors for the 21st Century

Lauren Ruth

EVERYDAY ETIQUETTE

ISBN: 9781798520284

DEDICATION

This book was written in loving memory of my grandmother, Catherine Elizabeth Tabor, née Slade. She was the classiest, most elegant woman I knew.

CONTENTS

Acknowledgments

I need to thank my aunt, Catherine Kielski, née Tabor who tells me there is nothing I can't do and how proud she is of me every day. I love you! I need to thank my son, Parys, as well. Every day he tells me "I'm so proud of you, Mommy." There is nothing that makes me smile more.

EVERYDAY ETIQUETTE

"Every Action done in Company, ought to be with Some Sign of respect, to those that are Present." – George Washington's "Rules of Civility and Decent Behaviour in Company and Conversation."

EVERYDAY ETIQUETTE

Introduction

In today's day and age, etiquette has regrettably become a thing of the past, something passé and seldom referred to. However, I believe there is no reason for bad manners and that it is never too late to learn how to behave appropriately. Let me be your etiquette coach and with the help of simple dos and don'ts teach you how to conduct yourself properly so that you make yourself more at ease and others around you comfortable no matter the situation.

EVERYDAY ETIQUETTE

Manners vs. Etiquette

There is a thin line between etiquette and manners. In this book, I am going to discuss what I believe to be good etiquette practices, but it's crucial to understand manners, as well. Having good manners means holding a door open for someone, helping a senior with their bags, or offering someone water on a hot day. Good manners mean showing human kindness, compassion and an all-around consideration for your fellow man. Etiquette is a code of conduct helping you navigate in polite society. However, manners and etiquette often share the same rules and behaviors, for example, the simple gestures that we take for granted, such as saying, "excuse me," "please" and "thank you" are polite and well-mannered, but also basic etiquette.

I want you to put yourself in this situation: someone is trying to get past you; if that person were to say, "excuse me, please" followed by a "thank you," you're much more likely to scoot over and let them by with a smile. Now think of yourself in the same situation, but the person rudely says "move!" Your demeanor will be altogether different, and you will probably even tell your loved ones about the ill-mannered person.

Although this book is about etiquette, it's important to understand that in the manners vs. etiquette debate, manners always wins. Not everyone knows who to introduce first, but anyone with good manners knows to be kind and polite when meeting someone new. I would never be offended if someone introduced people in the wrong order, but I would be appalled if someone were to make fun of another person's name in their presence. My grandmother used to say, "Etiquette matters, but manners matter more."

Why Practice Etiquette?

We have become desensitized to the world around us; this includes each other. People have become so engrossed in themselves that they forget they share the world with millions of other people. How many dates have you been on where the person spent more time looking at their iPhone than they spent looking at you? How many people have you seen checking Facebook in a dark movie theater? When was the last time you were in a car with someone who wasn't texting? These are basic etiquette faux pas. You're probably wondering what makes these etiquette faux pas. The simple answer is that etiquette is about making the people around you more comfortable. Therefore, we use the correct fork, chew with our mouths closed and put our phones away. You may wonder who is made more comfortable by these behaviors, so allow me to explain. By using the correct fork, you prevent people from watching you struggle to stab a steak with a small salad fork. When you chew with your mouth closed, you ensure that no one must see your chewed-up food and you prevent choking, which can be fatal. And of course, when you put your phone away, you ensure that your company feels worthy of your time and they yours. Your company will feel more comfortable and at ease and you will be able to carry yourself with pride and high self-esteem.

As you can see, etiquette is not some archaic system of behavior. They are simple rules that are used to make life a more enjoyable experience for everyone involved. The point is to make sure you are comfortable with your behavior and that others are comfortable being around you. Now that you have the why of it, I hope you are ready to learn the basics of etiquette and begin your journey into refinement.

Who Benefits From Etiquette?

EVERYONE! There is not a person alive who would not benefit from the use of proper etiquette. All one needs to do is think about their daily life. What makes you tick? What is something you've seen others do that makes you cringe? If you can think of something, then it is probably a breach of etiquette. Etiquette is about respect and it simply comes down to this: if you don't like it, then other people won't like it either.

8

Who Am I?

I wasn't raised in a large house on the shore with staff at my every beck and whim. I grew up in a modest home in central Connecticut. My family was happy and healthy. We didn't really struggle financially, but we weren't wealthy either. My father was a truck driver and my mother was a bartender, who went to nursing school when I was in high school. They did their best to give me a good upbringing and I think I turned out alright.

Even though I loved my parents, it was my paternal grandparents I admired and looked up to. My grandmother was my idol and I wanted nothing more than to be like her one day. I wanted her class, her style, and her seamless level of sophistication.

I was often around my grandmother and thanks to her, I learned to live with grace and style and a level of sophistication. I don't believe there is any need to take formal etiquette training, although I have benefitted from it myself. Rather than waste this arsenal of information, I want to help others.

Cell Phone Etiquette

Thanks to cell phones we have become more connected than we ever were before, but with that connection, there is an ever growing disconnect. It's important to learn the whys and the whens of cell phone use. When you aren't sure, put yourself in your company's shoes and imagine how you would feel on the other end. No longer will you be getting annoyed glances from others and hopefully everyone you encounter reads this book, and you won't have to give any annoyed glances in return.

Turn off your phone while at a theater, church, temple, weddings, funerals, etc. If you are expecting a call that you absolutely must take, keep your phone on silent or vibrate and step outside while on the phone. It is also important to keep these emergency calls short.

Don't use your phone while driving! It is dangerous! PERIOD.

Don't take phone calls on public transportation; it's just plain rude.

Watching videos and listening to music on your phone is a wonderful way to pass the time while on a bus, or on a walk or run, but be sure to use your headphones. Not everyone wants to hear your music or video.

Put your phone away while on a date. It's you and your partner; it's not you, your partner and two cell phones.

Don't text while you're with other people. Work and emergencies are the exceptions, just be sure to give an apology.

Keep sensitive conversations face to face. No one should be dumped in a text or be told of a death in the family over the phone.

Don't shout into the phone. It's modern technology, the party on the other end can hear you just fine. If it's windy, tell them you'll call them back when you're inside, they'll understand and appreciate it.

Return your missed calls with a call! Nothing makes someone feel inadequate like a missed call answered with a text.

Return a dropped call immediately.

Don't drunk call or text. You will probably say something you regret. This is especially dangerous if you have a boss on your phone.

Never hang up in anger.

Don't play on your phone during business meetings. It's terribly rude and unprofessional.

Please don't talk on your phone while you're using the bathroom. You can browse Facebook and Instagram until the moment you flush, but no one wants to hear you going number 2 or tinkling. Ignore the call, you can just call them back.

Answer the phone with a polite "hello" or "'your name' speaking". It should never be answered with "What's up?", "Talk to me" or "Yo." You never know who might be on the other line.

14

EVERYDAY ETIQUETTE

Dining Etiquette

Everyone eats. I want to make sure your experience is fantastic for you and your fellow diners whether you are at a restaurant, entertaining or a guest in someone else's home. Certain things are better shown to you in person, but here we will touch upon the basics.

Place your napkin in your lap, use it to wipe your hands and dab your face. Never wipe your face and never lick/suck on your fingers. If you excuse yourself from the table, place your napkin on your seat.

Don't wear your hat at the table unless you are a woman wearing a fascinator or fashionable/decorative hat (think Royal wedding and Kentucky Derby), you are ill and need your hat on your head for your comfort, or you are eating outdoors.

Always pass the salt and pepper together, even though most people only ask for one of the spices.

Don't talk with your mouth full of food! Please! No one will understand you and pieces will come flying out of your mouth. It's gross for everyone involved. It's also dangerous for you; you could choke.

Always start from the outside and work your way in using utensils. If the salad fork is to the left of the dinner fork, it means salad is coming after the meal. Just stick to the arrangement.

If you get a little confused over which is your bread plate and your cup, there is a little trick. Take both your hands making the standard ok sign, thus creating a 'b' and a 'd' with your hands. The 'b' side is where your bread plate will be and the 'd' side is where your drink will be.

Once your utensils have been touched, they should not be placed on the table again. If you take a break from eating, put them on your plate in the shape of an X. When you are finished eating, put both your knife and fork on your plate in the 5:00 position.

Always use a fork and knife unless it is finger food.

Use chopsticks to eat sushi. If you are a lady there is no exception to this rule, gentlemen, however, may use their hands.

Don't pick your teeth! I know some restaurants offer toothpicks, but they are not meant to be utilized at the table, excuse yourself to the restroom.

Ladies should keep their beauty secrets a secret! You shouldn't apply makeup or fix your hair at the table. Excuse yourself to the restroom.

Inform your host/hostess/server of any food allergies.

Don't slurp your soup or drink. In certain countries, this is acceptable etiquette and even expected, but in the Western world, it is a no-go.

Don't tip your soup bowl. It does not matter how delicious the soup was, you are just going to have to leave that last little bit behind.

Spoon your soup away from you. If you have never eaten your soup like this, it may take some getting used to, but the chances of spilling are less likely.

When you are a guest in someone's home, try to taste all the food on your plate before seasoning, otherwise, you are insinuating you don't trust the cook. Also, be sure to taste everything on your plate, even if it's usually something you don't like.

Chew with your mouth closed and thoroughly. No one wants to see your mashed-up food, and I assume you do not want to choke.

If you must belch, try to use the restroom, if an accident occurs, simply say "excuse me" and forget it happened.

Don't put your phone on the table. It's a silent message letting your company know that the phone takes precedence over anything else.

Pass dishes to the right (counterclockwise). However, if the person immediately to your left asks for something within reach, it is acceptable to hand it to them.

Don't reach over the table, politely ask for whatever you need.

If you are hosting a dinner party, please make sure your dishes, especially glassware and silverware are free of spots.

Don't put your elbows on the table when there is food. However, it is perfectly acceptable to put your elbows on the table while talking and during coffee.

Don't spit bones or bad tasting food into your napkin. You should discreetly put it on your fork and then put it on the side of your dish.

Don't pickoff someone else's plate. If you want to try their food, ask first.

It is considered rude to butter your entire piece of bread or roll. Just take the amount of butter you need and then butter each bite you take.

Don't turn your glass upside down. If you do not want any more to drink, put your fingers over the glass and tell the server, "no thank you."

Please don't ever stick your pinky finger out. "When in doubt pinky out" is not a real rule. It's considered rude. Your fingers should all be curled in toward you, no matter how small the cup/mug is.

After stirring coffee or tea, put your spoon down on the saucer, tea bag rest or a napkin, not on the table or table cloth. You should also never bang it on the side of the cup/mug or put it in your mouth to taste test and don't put it in the sugar dish. This spoon is strictly for stirring.

Spilling your drink it not poor etiquette, accidents happen. Etiquette is being gracious enough to understand that.

Brunch

The weekend is how we recuperate from our work week, but Sunday brunch is how we recuperate from the weekend. It consists of light breakfast and lunch fare usually served between 10:00 AM and 2:00 PM.

If there is alcohol being served, do not get drunk.

Stick to the available brunch menu. This is not the time to order dinner; if you want dinner, come back in the evening.

Do not skimp on the tip. Brunch is very popular and as a result, very busy. These servers deserve to be treated well for giving you great service.

Brunch is a great way to catch up with your friends about their week; but if there is a line of people waiting and you are done eating, it is best to continue your conversation elsewhere.

Keep the conversation light. No need to talk about politics or the news.

If you haven't seen your brunch companions in a while, it is best to put your phone away. They will feel unimportant compared to your phone.

Due to the busyness of brunch, consider paying with cash rather than trying to split up the meal between several cards.

Brunch can be held in one's home. Serve coffee, tea, and at least one 'breakfasty' alcoholic drink such as Mimosas, Screwdrivers, or Bloody Marys. Keep the fare light, but include both sweet and savory; buy or make muffins, scones, bagels, quiche, etc.

Weddings

Weddings are a joyous occasion, and it is an honor being invited to share in the happy couple's joy. Although these are happy occasions full of fun, dancing and sometimes even drinking, it's important to behave appropriately – you don't want the couple to remember you in a negative light when the reminiscence about their special day.

For the guest:

Be sure to RSVP. It's terribly rude not to let the couple know you are coming. Seating charts can take days, sometimes weeks of preparation, and showing up unexpectedly can add extra stress for the couple. There is also a respond by date, respect it.

Inform the couple of any food allergies so they can accommodate you.

Don't wear white, cream or ivory. These colors are reserved for the bride(s) and sometimes the groom(s).

Dress well; it's respectful to you and to the couple. But be sure to check the dress code, if there isn't one, it's best to go with traditional attire (dark/neutral suit and tie for gentlemen and a cocktail dress for ladies.) However, if the couple requests beach attire and you are in a wool suit or a black evening gown, you may look fantastic, but you will stick out like a sore thumb.

Don't say or do anything rude or disrespectful. And don't get drunk, you risk making a spectacle of yourself.

Respect the religious and cultural practices of the couple and their families. If the couple is devout and opts for a religious ceremony, be sure to observe the rules of etiquette. If you are asked for cover your head, or the couple asks that you dress modestly, etc. be kind enough to honor it. If you aren't sure what's expected, it's perfectly fine to call the church, synagogue, mosque, etc. to ask what is appropriate.

Don't skip the wedding ceremony! A wedding is a happy occasion, and everyone loves a party, but showing up to just the reception and not the wedding itself is a no-no.

Bring a wedding gift, even if you have already given a shower, engagement or bachelor/bachelorette gift. If you can't afford to buy a gift, a card with your congratulations is acceptable, showing up empty-handed is not.

Don't bring an unexpected guest. Speak to the couple about adding a plus one, etc.

Don't be late! If the ceremony starts at 5:00 PM, you should be there no later than 4:55 PM and even that is pushing it. If you think you can walk into the service at 5:10 PM, be prepared for many disgruntled looks.

Silence your phone, or better still, turn it off and put it away. Taking pictures with a phone may be okay – check with the couple first – but your phone should not be chiming during the ceremony.

Don't text the bride or the groom during their wedding. They have probably read this book and know their phone should be put away!

Don't make an unexpected speech. It may look great in the movies, but, it can cause embarrassment, hold off plans, and even cause other people to give unplanned speeches. If you really want to say something, feel free to speak to the couple beforehand.

No one should be chatting during the ceremony. It is acceptable to speak in the church before the ceremony starts, but once people are walking down the aisle, it should be quiet.

Please don't viciously fight for the bouquet/garter. It's meant to be lighthearted fun.

No matter your relation to the happy couple, you should never ask the couple if/when they are having kids.

Don't take over the dance floor.

Remember to have fun!

For the happy couple:

I know you're excited, but, share news of your engagement with family and close friends before posting on social media.

Don't be a Bride/Groomzilla!

Send out save the date cards and wedding invitations promptly.

Send an invitation to people who are special to you, and you want them to share in your day. Even if you know they can't attend, send the invitation anyway. It may become a special keepsake.

Don't feel the need to invite everyone you know. Keep it simple if you prefer; this is your day.

Invite family groups equally. You can't invite one aunt and not the others. Be prepared to invite all the aunts and uncles or let your favorite aunt know you will just be having an intimate ceremony.

Do not invite someone to your engagement/shower/bachelor/bachelorette party and not to your wedding. This will give cause for hurt feelings that may last for years.

Never invite a guest through email or social media. Wedding invitations should only be sent through traditional mail.

It is extremely rude to send your registry with your invitation. This is basically telling everyone, "You're invited if you bring something." You can create a wedding Facebook page or even a wedding site with information about your registry. You can include the website information on your invitations.

Consider all your guests when creating a menu. Are there any vegetarians? Someone with gluten sensitivity? Guests should know to inform you of any allergies.

Call anyone who has not sent an RSVP by your deadline. It could have gotten lost in the mail. Do not assume they just did not bother to respond.

Never uninvite anyone, even if they are rude or criticizing. There are extenuating circumstances to uninviting guests, such as the venue flooded or caught on fire and the reception needs to be downsized your parents' home.

Feel free to wear whatever color you want. Although white is traditional for brides, this is your day. If you want to wear a purple dress, do it! Just be forewarned, guests know not to wear white and compete with the bride, but if you choose a non-traditional color, odds are someone else may also be wearing it.

Don't touch your phone during your wedding! Take some selfies and make some posts while getting ready for the wedding, but once the wedding has started, it should never be in your hands.

Don't have guests pay for their own drinks. A bar is going to cost you money but setting up a cash bar is rude.

Send out handwritten thank you cards. This will be time-consuming, there is no way around it. But, a guest receiving a card that was tailored to them makes it all worthwhile. There is no need to get too extravagant, you can write something as simple as: "Thank you for joining us on our special day. We especially love the crockpot. We will be making many delicious meals in it."

Try to send out all your thank you cards no later than 2-3 months after the wedding.

Give your bridesmaids and groomsmen special gifts. It took a lot of time, money and effort for them to be a part of your big day; it is kind to thank them properly.

You paid your vendors, but don't forget to feed them! Your officiant, your DJ or band, your wedding planner, your photographer, etc. were all part of making your day a huge success don't treat them poorly.

30

Wedding Showers

The wedding shower is a small party for the bride, thrown by her bridesmaids and/or her close female relatives or soon to be in laws. It is traditionally women only and gifts are usually given to the bride.

Don't invite anyone who isn't invited to the wedding. If they are going to the shower they are going to the wedding, period. Usually close female relatives of the bride(s) or groom are invited. Close friends can also be invited.

Invitations should be sent by mail, not through email or social media. Be sure to include the bride's name, date, time and location and registry information. You can also include the host's information for RSVP and whether or not it's a surprise.

Invitations should be mailed out four to six weeks before the event. The event should take place one to four months before the wedding.

Don't assume it's only for first time brides. Any woman getting married can have a shower thrown in her honor.

Remember the bride when planning! A theme is not necessary, but you can theme it around her favorite movie, book, TV show, color, etc. It does not have to match her wedding theme.

You can have an extravagant event, or something simple in the backyard. Consider your budget. The bride will appreciate the gesture either way.

Plan some games with some prizes. It will get dull if everyone is just sitting around talking. People don't have to join in if they don't want to.

Be sure to RSVP if you are invited!

If there is no registry, consider something she can use in her new home.

Do not buy lingerie or sexual toys. These are inappropriate and can be embarrassing for the bride.

Brides, be sure to write thank you cards!

34

Baby Showers

Baby showers are a time to celebrate the coming of new life with an expectant mother. It is also a great way to help the new mom with necessities or with larger items she may need help with getting.

Traditionally baby showers were women only events and you can feel free to keep it that way, but today both men and women are welcome to celebrate a new life.

Any close family or friends can host the baby shower.

Don't feel the need to make it extravagant. Something small in someone's home with some finger food is perfect.

Be sure to mail the invitations in a timely manner. Do not send invitations via email or social media. The only exception to the email rule is if a shower is thrown by co-workers for an expectant mother.

Add some fun games with some prizes, you don't want people to feel bored.

Baby showers aren't just for pregnant moms, they can be for adoptive moms, moms with surrogates or even adoptive dads! Celebrating a new family member is all inclusive.

The best time to host a baby shower is in the second trimester. The mom is still able to walk comfortably but she is past the uncertainty of the first trimester.

Do not serve food that makes the expectant mother nauseous or ill.

Don't bring up anything that may make the new

mom uncomfortable such as horrifying birth stories, breast feeding difficulties, stretch marks, dirty diapers, terrible twos, etc.

If you cannot afford a gift, offering to babysit is a wonderful option. Sometimes new parents just need a night to themselves – or a nap! Just be sure to honor the offer. (If you are the new parents, do not take advantage of people willing to help you with babysitting.)

Housewarming Parties

A housewarming party is a small, casual affair to celebrate a new home. Sometimes gifts are given for the new home owner(s) to start their new chapter.

Host:

Do not host a housewarming for a new apartment, unless it is your first apartment. Even if you do, do not expect gifts or create a registry.

Do not host a housewarming party with boxes all over the place; make sure your new home is presentable.

Offer tours of your new home or ask a close family member to do so.

This is usually a small, casual event, but feel free to make it extravagant if you want.

Do not cook a lavish meal. Some finger foods and drinks are ideal.

Send out invitations by mail no later than a week before the event.

If you receive gifts, do not open them until your guests leave.

Be sure to send thank you cards to all your guests.

Guest:

When coming to a housewarming, a gift should be brought. It doesn't have to be the most expensive dish set you could find, it can be something as simple as a bottle of wine or a bouquet of flowers.

Give your gift with discretion; it's not a competition over who spent the most money. Leave your gift in the area with other gifts.

If you bring someone with you, be sure to introduce them to the host upon entering.

Be sure to compliment on the host's new home.

Do not make a negative comment. Something as simple as "What a small bathroom" can really hurt someone.

Do not hog the host! Talk and mingle with the other guests. This is a great time to make new acquaintances.

Upon leaving, remember to thank your host and compliment their new home once again.

Wakes, Funerals and Memorials

Unfortunately, death is a reality of this world. Everything that is born must die. This is a difficult time, and you may wish to extend your condolences and sympathies; but, it's important to remember that there is an etiquette to funerals and it needs to be respected for the comfort of the grievers.

Send a sympathy card. Even if you attend the wake or funeral, a card is still welcome.

You can send flowers or make donations in the deceased's name to their favorite charity.

Don't attend if you feel your presence will make the family uncomfortable or it is clearly a private event.

Arrive at the funeral or memorial on time. Wakes are like an open house, and people may come and go for several hours, whereas funerals and memorials have a designated time. You honor the deceased by arriving on time.

Respect the religious and cultural customs of the deceased and their family. If you are unsure, call the church, synagogue, mosque, etc. to ask. You may even be able to call the funeral home. However, don't feel obligated to pray if you are of another faith, simply sit quietly.

Wear a dark color; black, navy blue and even gray are acceptable. Only wear a bright color if it is requested of the family, such as the deceased's favorite color should be worn, it is requirement of their religious beliefs, etc.

Sign the guest book if there is one. It will let the family know you came and what your relationship was with the deceased.

Offer condolences to the entire receiving line, even

if you don't know everyone

Don't drink before the wake or funeral. Your presence should bring the family some comfort, not an embarrassment.

Don't sit in the front two rows if you are not immediate family. I should also note that once you find your seat, you should stay there. Far too often I have seen people playing musical chairs during a wake, it's distracting and impolite.

Offer to help in any way. Even if the family says "no, thank you," it will mean a lot knowing that you care.

Don't bring food or drinks into the funeral home. If you are hungry, eat before you get there.

Put your phone away.

Don't smoke in the funeral home. There is probably a designated smoking area outside.

Giving food to the deceased's family is a kind gesture. If you do offer food, be sure it is home-cooked. A pie from the grocery store just isn't as meaningful.

Share happy memories. Thinking happy thoughts helps the grieving process.

Never bad mouth the deceased. This is not the time to air out your dirty laundry or unresolved issues.

Don't take pictures; this is a solemn occasion. There may be exceptions to this rule based on the cultural practices of the deceased or the deceased's family. If that is the case, it is best to check with the family or funeral home first.

Don't walk on other headstones/foot-stones while at the cemetery, if you can help it. This is someone's loved one as well, and they deserve your respect.

Never spit, chew gum, smoke, drink, eat or touch your phone while in the cemetery.

Don't let children run around the cemetery like it's a playground. A burial ground is sacred, and many people will be perturbed with your children's behavior and yours.

If you are a member of the deceased's immediate family send out handwritten thank you cards to everyone who signed the guestbook, sent flowers or donated to a charity in the deceased's name.

Baptisms

Most religions offer some form of baptism. A baptism is a joyous occasion celebrating someone's dedication or devotion to God – by whatever name(s) you use. Whether adult or child, an invitation should be met with respect and as a happy, meaningful celebration.

Respect the religious and cultural customs of the family. They wanted you here for such a spiritual experience for a reason. Show them your gratitude with kindness and understanding.

Don't text or make a call during the ceremony. This is a paramount day for the family; it should be treated as such by you as well.

Arrive on time. This a joyful but serious occasion and needs to be treated as such.

Dress conservatively. You are going to be in a place of worship.

RSVP. The family needs to know how many people will attend to accommodate for seating and food.

Don't feel the need to bring a gift, although they will be welcomed. If you do decide to bring a gift, make sure it is appropriate for the occasion, i.e., a bible, a silver spoon, a picture frame, a keepsake box, etc.

Don't expect an extravagant meal. The food served is usually light fare such as juice, coffee, finger foods, etc.

Bar/Bat Mitzvahs

Bar/Bat Mitzvahs are coming of age ceremonies for Jewish children (13 for boys, 12 for girls). They are now regarded as adults and have more responsibility to God and the community. This a happy occasion and if you were invited, consider yourself lucky; this is a fun day.

RSVP. These can be big celebrations with many people, and the family needs to know who is coming.

Arrive on time.

Don't arrive late, unless you want every eye in the synagogue on you.

Dress conservatively. You will be in a house of worship.

Respect the religious and cultural customs of the family. This may mean covering your head.

Don't gossip with friends or other guests during the ceremony, or you will be shushed.

Don't text or talk on your phone. It should be turned off or at least silent/on vibrate.

Throw the candy when it's time. Yes, throw the candy. It is to symbolize that life is sweet.

Bring an appropriate gift. Money in multiples of 18 is considered good luck.

Don't smoke! This is not allowed on Shabbat. If you absolutely MUST have a cigarette, wait until you are at the party afterward and even then, be sure to smoke outside in a designated area.

Try to follow along.

Don't feel embarrassed if you are having a hard time following because you don't practice Judaism. No one is judging you. The family invited you because you are important to them, so don't worry if you make a mistake. You can always ask someone next to you where you are in the prayer/ceremony. They will be happy to help you.

Don't get drunk. There will probably be drinking for the "real" adults, but this is not an invitation to embarrass yourself or the family.

Say "Shabbat Shalom" or "Mazel Tov" rather than "Happy Birthday." This isn't just any birthday, this the birthday.

52

Sweet Sixteen

The sixteenth birthday is a big deal for girls and they usually throw a large and extravagant party. Although it is traditionally a celebration of a girl's coming of age, there is nothing wrong with throwing something similar for a boy. In Hispanic culture, a Quinceañera (the fifteenth birthday) is celebrated, but the etiquette is the same for both.

Be sure to RSVP, these parties can range from simple affairs to extravagant galas and the event planner will rely on a headcount.

You should dress well, but much like a wedding, don't upstage the young lady on her birthday. She will most likely wear a formal evening gown.

Buy gifts based on what the young lady (or gentleman) likes and on what the parents allow. Money, gift cards and jewelry are typical gifts. Personalized gifts are extremely thoughtful and may become sentimental items that can be handed down to her future children and grandchildren.

If you are an adult, watch the teenagers diligently, but try not to hover.

While you should not hover, it is also important to give the birthday girl (boy) their due attention. Remember to wish them a 'Happy Birthday.'

If there is alcohol at the party, it should only be for those 21 or over and no one should be drunk. As the adults, you should be setting an example.

After the party, the newly sixteen-year-old lady (or gentleman) should send out handwritten thank you cards to each of her guests, regardless of whether they bought you a gift or not.

Public Transportation

I am a huge advocate of public transportation. I use it myself! I think it is eco-friendly, cheaper than owning a car, and a safe way to nap before/after work. More and more people see the benefits of public transportation, and it's becoming more common. If you plan on utilizing it, there are certain rules and guidelines necessary to make traveling more comfortable for yourself and others.

Sit if there is a seat available. If there is no seat available, hold on to the available handles. You want to avoid falling on someone.

Don't talk on the phone. If you must, keep your conversations brief. Between the noise of the bus or train, other people talking, etc. it may be hard to hear the other person which can cause discomfort for the other passengers listening to you shout and to the party on the other side of the phone.

Offer your seat to the elderly, the disabled, pregnant women and young children.

Don't eat on the bus. I only mention eating because it can get very messy. I believe bringing a coffee with you on your morning commute or a bottle of water on a hot day is acceptable if you are responsible and avoid spills or dropping your drink. No one likes to be smacked in the ankle by a runaway bottle when the bus stops.

Be respectful of others and their space.

Wear deodorant. This is tight quarters, and no one wants to smell you. If you have a sweat problem, and many people do, carry a travel size deodorant with you for reapplying.

Don't over-share. It's great to strike up a conversation with a stranger, and you may even make a new friend, but be mindful; your brand-new friend may not want to hear about your new rash.

Wear headphones. It's great to listen to music, an audiobook, or watch your shows/movies but not everyone may want to join you.

Don't sing out loud. If you want to become the next big music artist, I'll happily buy your first album, but I don't want to hear your attempts at 9 AM on my way to work.

Bring a book. I'm a huge advocate of reading. I think the morning commute is a great time to catch up on some light-hearted reading.

Don't stare. There can be some interesting characters on public transportation, that absolutely does not mean it is appropriate to stare at them.

Please don't pop your gum. This is one of my biggest pet peeves. I do NOT want to hear you constantly pop your gum during the entirety of the ride. Please don't smack it either. If you have an oral fixation, switch to hard candies or mints.

Gym

Many people have learned the benefit of exercise, and while you can exercise at home, some people prefer the gym. The gym is a public and shared area, so it's important to be mindful of others and be respectful of others.

Follow the rules of the gym.

Pay your membership bill on time. You don't want to be in a situation where you're checking in, but you can't because your account hasn't been paid.

Clean the equipment after you are done; other people will be using it.

Don't loudly grunt and groan as you lift weights. No one is impressed.

Don't block the mirror. It's there for a reason, and if you want to use it, surely other people do as well.

It's terribly rude to steal a machine. If you see a towel or water bottle there, it's probably being used. Wait a few minutes before deciding to just move it out of your way.

Use headphones to listen to music. Music is great to keep a fast pace, but others may not want to hear it.

Put weights/other equipment away when you're done. No one should have to go searching for things because you didn't put them back.

Don't drop the weights; certain gyms even have alarms for that.

Don't ruin the equipment by using it wrong or storing it wrong. Items in the gym are quite expensive.

Don't stare at others. It's just creepy, even if you don't mean it to be. If you need help with something, the staff will be happy to assist you.

Shower! No need to walk around smelling like onions.

Business

Most of us work, it is necessary for our survival, and we are at our jobs up to 8 hours a day, if not more. When you are working so closely with people for so long, it is imperative to treat everyone there with respect and dignity, including yourself.

Do your job! You aren't getting paid to sit on social media while everyone else around you is picking up your slack.

Don't use company time to do personal projects. If you are given a long enough lunch break, work on it then.

Respect your co-workers!

Don't bad mouth your boss or your company on social media. Someone may see it, and it can affect your job.

Don't gossip about co-workers to other employees, this creates discomfort for many people and leaves people feeling like they are in high school, not in a professional setting.

Don't lie to get ahead. Eventually, your lies will catch up to you.

Wear your uniform properly. If there isn't a uniform, dress with professionalism in mind. This means gentlemen should be wearing a button-down shirt and tie with dark/neutral slacks or khakis. Hair should be neat and trimmed. Shave! If you prefer facial hair, be sure it is also neat and trimmed. Ladies have some extra options, dresses, skirts, pants with a nice top or a button down, a blazer or cardigan is also a great option. Just be sure that you aren't showing cleavage or wearing a mini skirt. Jewelry should be toned down, as should your makeup and hair.

Arrive on time. Your employer is counting on you and paying you for your time. You must honor that.

Don't come to work if you are ill.

Walk with your head high and your shoulders back. Slouching gives the impression of laziness!

Life happens, but you should call if you are going to be late.

Honor deadlines. They were given for a reason.

Attend business meetings.

Don't play on your phone or have side conversations during a meeting or presentation. The person speaking deserves your utmost respect.

Let people know if they are on speakerphone and who they will be speaking to.

When making a call, let people know who they are talking to and what company/branch you work in.

Respect everyone at the company. The janitor deserves just as much respect as the manager.

It's very inconsiderate to drink all the coffee and never refill the pot or buy coffee related products. When there is an office coffee machine, it is everyone's responsibility to pitch in.

Don't microwave fish or other smelly foods at work; and, you make a mess in the break area, clean up after yourself.

Never steal company property/merchandise/etc. It's unethical, and at the end of the day, you are only stealing from yourself.

Don't break the rules for particular customers/patrons.

Follow safety rules and protocol.

Have fun and make friends. You are going to see these people quite often; it's best if you aren't walking into enemy territory daily.

Interviews

It is rare for a job to hire you sight unseen, so an interview is a required step into a position. This is when you put your best foot forward and let your future employer know why you would be an asset to their company.

Arrive on time, or better yet, a few minutes early. Showing up late to an interview shows a lack of responsibility.

Dress your best. I can't stress this enough. I have seen people go to an interview in jeans or sneakers. You don't need to spend a fortune on your outfit, but it needs to be professional, neat and clean. Dress as if you were giving a presentation to colleagues, because you are presenting yourself to future colleagues.

Shake hands with a firm, not tight grip and two pumps of the hand will do.

If you aren't sure how to pronounce someone's name, ask.

Do not use first names unless the interviewer does so first.

Pay attention and focus. I know it can be nerve wracking and your mind may wander, but pay close attention. They may ask you a question or give you information about the position that you may need later.

Don't ask what the pay is until the interviewer asks you if you have any questions. It is rude to ask at the beginning of the interview.

No matter the position, write a thank you letter a day or two after the interview. If you write it any sooner than that, you might come off as desperate. Although actual mail is the most proper, it might not reach the employer in time, so an email is best. Sometimes this makes all the difference in being considered for the position.

If you decide not to take a job, let the employer know through an email or phone call and be sure to thank them for the opportunity.

Dating

Dating is an exciting time no matter your age. Treating others with respect is basic human decency that should extend into the realms of dating. These are helpful dos and don'ts for the first date.

Respect the other person and their comfort level. If you sense any kind of discomfort by an advance, then it is unwelcome, that means to remove your hand from theirs, remove your arm from around their shoulders, etc.

Pay if you are the man. It sounds old-fashioned and it is, but these are the rules. Once a relationship has been established, it becomes much more equal. As for same-sex dating, the person who initiated the date should be the one who pays. Both parties should know who is paying from the beginning to avoid any awkwardness; it can ruin the entire feel of the date and prevent the second one.

Arrive on time! I know I have mentioned this several times throughout this book and I cannot stress it enough.

Dress to impress. A date is your time to shine and show what kind of person you are really. Clothing can make or break an impression; showing up in sloppy clothing shows how little you care.

Don't text or use social media while on a date. Continually using your phone instead of talking sends an unspoken message that you are bored or uninterested.

Don't judge. You are nervous, and they are nervous, there's going to be some awkwardness, some bad jokes and maybe even a spill or two. Let it go.

Don't get drunk. You will ruin your chances of a second date.

Don't swear. You need to be on your best behavior.

Don't bring up past relationships or unpleasant dates, complain about your job, talk about how much work your car needs, the difficulties of potty training your dog, etc.

Do not talk politics or religion.

Think outside the box. There is no need to rely on the traditional route of dinner and movie; it can get dull. Consider some interesting alternatives: a museum, a play, a walk in the park, a coffee shop, a bookstore, the options are endless. Have fun and let your creativity shine.

If you are looking for something serious or long term, don't rush intimacy.

75

Break-Ups and Divorce

Unfortunately, in the world of dating and marriage, there is also break-ups and divorce. Sometimes our differences are so extreme that they can't be worked through; this doesn't make anyone failures or bad people, it just means the relationship has come to an end.

Understand that maybe no one is to blame. Sometimes these things happen, and they can end amicably.

Don't bad mouth your ex. It's just not nice.

It's cruel to make your friends choose sides. You might lose friends during the break-up and you might not, but making your friends choose only one of you puts everyone in an uncomfortable situation.

Be fair when splitting up assets or belongings. If his favorite college shirt means a lot to him, you should not lie to keep it (no matter how comfortable it is to sleep in), and you shouldn't throw it away.

Mourn. A breakup or divorce means a season of your life has come to an end; pain is normal, let it happen.

Accept that it is over. There's no need to text that you want them back or look for love spells to return a lost lover.

Don't try to be friends right away and avoid sleeping together. You will not be able to recover from the pain. Give yourself reasonable time to grieve, and maybe eventually the two of you can be friendly.

Consider your children, if you have any. No need to drag them into it. They are already going through a rough time.

Never share the intimate details of the break up on social media. The relationship was between two people, and the break up should be the same way.

Don't jump into a new relationship. In the end, it will have just been a rebound, and now more people will end up being hurt.

Clothing and Presentation

I thoroughly believe it is everyone's right to express themselves through fashion and style. No one should make you feel bad about what you want to wear. Despite this, I think everyone should dress in a way that makes others around them comfortable.

Wear clothing that makes you happy. At the end of the day, you're the one wearing it, not me.

Wear clothing that fits. It doesn't matter how much you spend, because whether you bought it at the thrift store or high-end department store, it makes no difference if the clothes don't fit you properly. This means clothing shouldn't be too tight. I can't tell you how many times I've seen a woman wearing clothes that are way too small and she can barely walk. It also shouldn't be too baggy. It looks unkept and careless.

Consider where you are going. Are you going to a house of worship? A wedding? Work? These are all thoughts that need to be addressed and you need to dress accordingly.

Consider wearing clothing that compliments your coloring. If you are cool, stick to cooler colors and if you are a warm, stick to warmer colors. This is just a suggestion, if you are a warm and love blue, wear it.

Avoid wearing low rise pants and creating a muffin top. No one likes it.

Don't show too much cleavage or leg ladies! Leave a little to the imagination.

Don't show your butt cracks, gentlemen! No one finds a plumber's crack sexy.

Is your clothing in good condition? Mend ripped clothing and replace missing buttons.

Gentlemen, dress like a gentleman; You will garner more respect if you do. This means not walking around in ripped clothing, pants hanging off your butt or a thin tank top. It's just not respectable.

Don't wear sandals with socks! Just don't do it. It looks ridiculous. And if you do wear sandals, make sure your feet are presentable; no one wants to see dead, peeling skin or long, yellow toenails.

Gentlemen, please avoid ties with ridiculous patterns or characters.

Ladies make sure your bra fits properly! Many stores offer free bra fittings.

No matter your gender, I should not be able to see your underwear!

If people can smell you after you leave the room, you are wearing too much cologne or perfume. Just a dab is all you need.

Do your best to always look presentable. This doesn't mean spending a fortune on your wardrobe. It means wearing clean, well-fitting clothes, keeping your shoes clean and making sure your hair is combed, your face is fresh, there's no dirt under your fingernails – which should also be trimmed. There is no second chance to make a first impression and you want the judgment to be made in your favor.

82

Always Remember:

Never speak about money with others, it's crass and insensitive.

Never ask a woman her age.

Avoid talking about religion or politics in social settings.

Never lend a borrowed book. When you do return it, include a handwritten thank you note.

While we all love a visitor, it is essential to give a phone call first, rather than just showing up. The person may be ill, underdressed, or on their way out.

A gentleman should always carry a lighter with him. You may need it to light a lady's cigarette or your father in law's cigar! It also serves as a light source in a pinch.

If you were invited to someone's home for dinner, a party, or a picnic you should bring something; flowers, candy, wine, beer, etc. They will appreciate the gesture.

And remember to send your host a handwritten thank you card within a week of the event.

When giving flowers to a hostess, be sure to bring them in a vase. It is an inconvenience to them to have to stop entertaining to find one.

If you think you may have offended someone, apologize.

Use a soft voice; there's no need to shout at people.

A gentleman should take a lady's coat, to check in or hang, but there is no reason that he should be holding her purse or pocketbook.

If you are with a friend or relative and they run into someone they know, you should also give a greeting, even if you don't know their friend.

Two wrongs do not make a right. If someone offends you, be the bigger person and turn the other cheek.

If you are driving and see people walking, slow down. You don't want to be the jerk who splashed them with water or got sand/dirt in their eyes.

When carrying a wet umbrella, lightly shake off excess water (away from other people) before entering a building and carry it so it does not poke anyone. Some stores offer umbrella bags, please utilize them.

If you are thinking of someone, send them a letter or

thinking of you card. It will be much more appreciated than a text message or email.

When walking on the sidewalk, stay to the right and keep moving. Please don't stop to look at your phone, if you must, then move to the side.

Remove sunglasses and headphones when speaking to someone.

Don't ask for someone's Wi-Fi password, unless you are staying with them for an extended period.

When writing any kind of correspondence (handwritten or email) be sure to use correct grammar.

Clean up after your dog. No one likes to step in feces.

Gentlemen do not smoke in front of a lady without asking her permission first.

Ladies, cross your legs at your ankles, with the feet tucked behind you. Do NOT cross your knees and NEVER sit with your legs open, I don't care if you are wearing pants or not. It's completely and utterly unladylike.

Gentlemen, please don't adjust yourself in public. Use the restroom for that.

If you need to change your baby's diaper in someone's home, ask for a comfortable place to do so.

The same goes for feeding, depending on your comfort level.

Be mindful of what you post on social media!

Ask before bringing your pet to someone else's home.

If someone is inviting you to an event in their home, you should never show up empty handed.

Don't slouch! Walk with your head high and your shoulders back; show the world you are proud of who you are!

Thank you notes should always be handwritten.

Always ARRIVE ON TIME!

87

I know that was a lot of information. Mastering etiquette is a work in progress and I wouldn't expect everyone to remember all this right away, but with practice and diligence you can do it. Mistakes happen and we learn from them.

88

ABOUT THE AUTHOR

Lauren Ruth is a native New Englander and a graduate of Bay Path University. When she is not brushing up on her etiquette, she is spending time with her family, reading, crafting or studying New England's rich history. To read more about etiquette, fashion and living the New England lifestyle, visit her blog anchorsbowsandclamchowder.wordpress.com.